At Home with Science

Listen and See!

What's on TV?

Written by Janice Lobb

Illustrated by Peter Utton and Ann Savage

KING*f*ISHER

NEW YORK

KINGFISHER
Larousse Kingfisher Chambers Inc.
95 Madison Avenue
New York, New York 10016
www.lkcpub.com

First published in 2001
10 9 8 7 6 5 4 3 2 1

1TR/1200/FR/SC/128JDA

Created and designed by Snapdragon Publishing Ltd
Copyright © Snapdragon Publishing Ltd 2001

LIBRARY OF CONGRESS CATALOGING-IN-PUBLICATION DATA
has been applied for.

ISBN 0-7534-5336-3

Printed in Hong Kong

For Snapdragon
Editorial Director Jackie Fortey
Art Director Chris Legee
Designers Chris Legee and Joy Fitzsimons

For Kingfisher
Series Editor Emma Wild
Series Art Editor Mike Davis
DTP Coordinator Nicky Studdart
Production Controller Debbie Otter

Contents

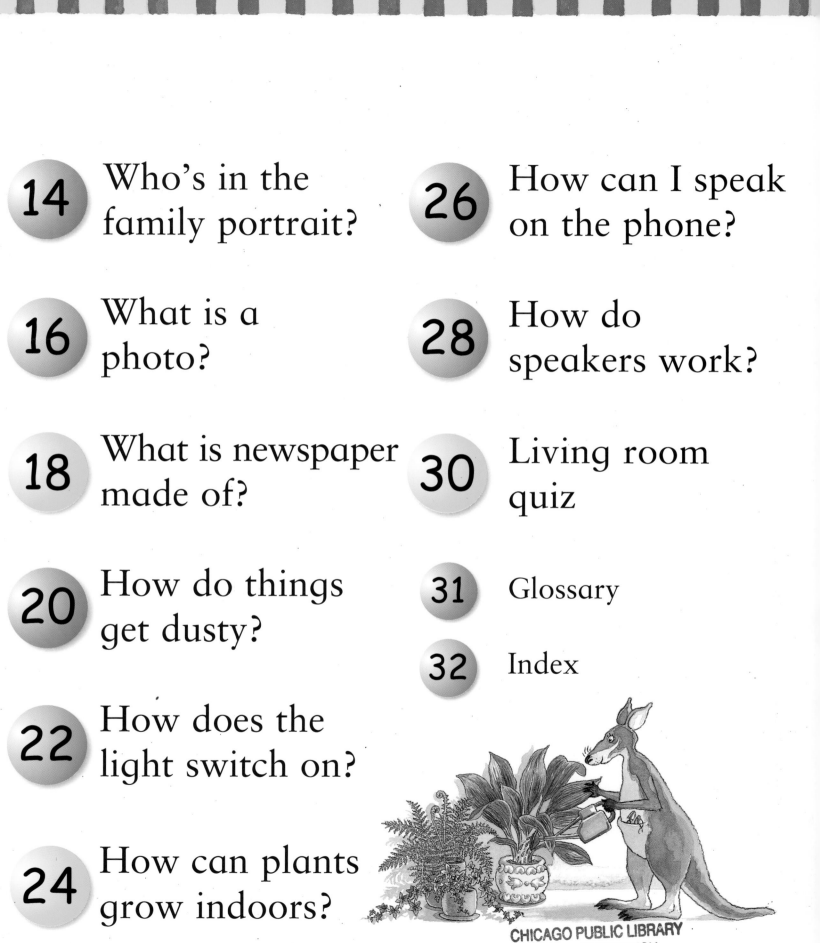

About this book

There's an amazing amount of science happening in your living room. Every time you turn on the TV, pick up the telephone, or bounce up and down on the sofa, exciting things begin to happen. This book tells you how to look around you, ask the right questions, and make your own discoveries about the science in your own home.

Why?

What if?

What?

Which?

How?

Where?

Hall of Fame

Archie and his friends are here to help you. They are each named after famous scientists—apart from Bob the (rubber) Duck, who is just a young scientist like you!

Archie
ARCHIMEDES (287–212 B.C.)
The Greek scientist Archimedes figured out why things float or sink while he was in the bathtub. According to the story, he was so pleased that he leaped up, shouting "Eureka!" which means "I've done it!"

Frank
BENJAMIN FRANKLIN (1706–1790)
Besides being one of the most important figures in American history, he was also a noted scientist. In a dangerous experiment in which he flew a kite in a storm, he proved that lightning is actually electricity.

Marie
MARIE CURIE (1867–1934)
Girls did not go to college in Poland where Marie Curie grew up, so she went to Paris to study. Later, she worked on radioactivity and received two Nobel prizes for her discoveries, in 1903 and 1911.

Dot
DOROTHY HODGKIN (1910–1994)
Dorothy Hodgkin was a British scientist who made many important discoveries about molecules and atoms, the tiny particles that make up everything around us. She was given the Nobel prize for Chemistry in 1964.

See for yourself!

1 Read about the science in your living room, then try the "See for yourself!" experiments to discover how it works. In science, experiments try to find or show the answers.

Battery

2 Carefully read the instructions for each experiment, making sure you follow the numbered instructions in the correct order.

3 Here are some of the things you will need. Have everything ready before you start each experiment.

Paper
Balloon
Rubber bands
Cardboard
Glue
Mirrors
Wood toy brick
Sandpaper
Bowl
Lamp
Battery
Flashlight bulb
Fuse wire
Tinfoil
Box
Plastic cups
Plant
String
Cookie sheet
Sequin
Thread
Cardboard tube
Flashlight
Magnifying glass
Tape
Frame
Colored cellophane
Mesh canvas
Colored pencils

4 # Safety first!

Some scientists took risks to make their discoveries, but our experiments are safe. Just make sure that you tell an adult what you are doing and ask them to help when you see the warning sign.

Amazing facts

WOW!

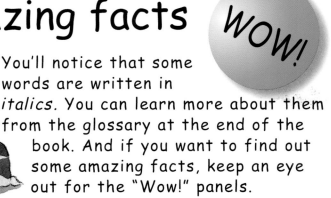

You'll notice that some words are written in *italics*. You can learn more about them from the glossary at the end of the book. And if you want to find out some amazing facts, keep an eye out for the "Wow!" panels.

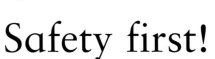
Keep an eye out for useful tips!

Have fun!

How does a TV screen work?

A TV screen is made of a special type of glass. The back of the glass is coated with little dots of a substance called *phosphor*. A color screen has three types of phosphor: red, green, and blue. When the TV is off, the screen looks black, but when it is on, the tiny phosphor dots glow in their colors. If the TV is not tuned in, you see small, white dots dancing around like a snowstorm. When the TV is *tuned* to a channel, the dots form a pattern, which our eyes see as a picture.

What does a duck like to watch on TV?

Duckumentaries!

Dotty pictures

There are three special electron guns inside the TV. They fire beams of tiny electric particles, called *electrons*, at the phosphor dots, making them glow.

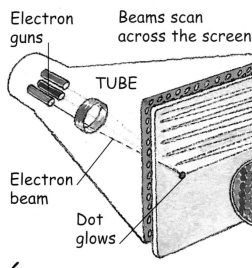

Electron guns

Beams scan across the screen

TUBE

Electron beam

Dot glows

Colored dots make up the picture

White dot

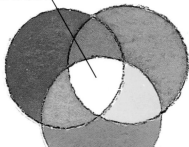

The phosphor dots are arranged in groups of three: one dot glows red, one green, and one blue. If they glow at the same time, we see a white dot.

When we see only red and green light together, we see yellow. Red and blue light make magenta, and blue and green make cyan.

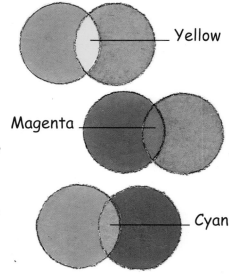

Yellow

Magenta

Cyan

See for yourself!

1 Tape some red cellophane (or polyethylene from a red plastic bag) over the end of a flashlight. Then shine it on a white wall. What color is the light?

Red cellophane

2 Cover two more flashlights with cellophane—one blue and one green. Shine them on the wall separately. What do you see?

Blue cellophane

Green cellophane

3 Now shine two of the flashlights, so that their beams overlap. What color do you see?

Red cellophane

Green cellophane

4 Then shine all three flashlights, so that their beams overlap. What color do you see?

Green cellophane

Red cellophane

?

Blue cellophane

Be careful—don't touch the back of your TV.

WOW! Color vision

Our eyes need to be able to sense red, blue, and green light to see all the colors coming from the screen. People who are color-blind usually cannot tell the difference between red and green.

Why is my sofa comfortable?

Some of us are happy to sit on the floor, but we usually prefer chairs, beanbags, or a nice comfortable sofa. Hard seats are not very comfortable, although molded, shaped seats feel better than flat ones. Padded seats and cushions have more "give." The foam or feathers inside them squash down when we sit on them because air is pushed out. The shape of the cushions changes to fit our shape, even if we move.

What did the chair say to the sofa?

You need a spring cleaning!

Storing energy

When you sit on a chair, your weight pushes down on the seat. The chair seat pushes back. If the chair is harder than you, your bottom gets squashed!

Springs and foam rubber compress instead of pushing back. They store *energy*.

When you get up, the springs use their stored energy to quickly spring back to their normal shape and size. We say springs and foam rubber are *elastic*.

Weight

Upward push from chair equals weight

Weight

Normal spring

Compressed springs store energy.

Energy helps springs get back into shape.

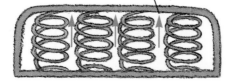

8

See for yourself!

 1 Try to dent the seat of a wood or plastic chair by pressing it with your finger. You are putting a *force* on the chair. It squashes the end of your finger, but not the chair!

Chair seat

2 Press your finger into a beanbag. You make a dent because the force pushes the beans out of the way. When you remove your finger, the dent stays there, because the beans cannot move back by themselves. A beanbag is not elastic.

Beanbag

3 Now try pressing down on springs or foam rubber. They also change shape under the force of your finger, but unlike the beans, they spring back again.

Sofa with springs

Style before comfort!

WOW!

Ouch!

In the past, the shape of seats changed with clothing fashions, both of which were not always comfortable. In the 1700s, some women wore such huge headdresses and wide skirts, it was hard for them to sit down at all!

Do not poke blown-up cushions too hard!

How do radiators work?

We often stand near a hot radiator to keep warm. Its heat is transferred to us in three ways. First, a radiator sends out *heat energy* toward us by *radiation*. Invisible waves of energy travel through air, like waves moving across the ocean. Second, if we touch a warm radiator, we get even more heat by *conduction*. Heat from inside the radiator passes through the metal to our hands. Finally, a radiator heats most of the room by *convection*.

Why doesn't anyone listen to the radiator?

It's full of hot air!

Convection

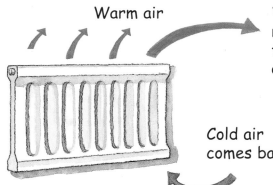

Warm air

Warm air reaches the far corners of a room.

Cold air comes back.

The air just above a hot radiator warms up. This makes it lighter, and it rises, taking heat energy with it. The air then comes down again farther away and warms a cooler part of the room.

Fire in the fireplace gives off light as well as heat, but a lot of its heat is lost up the chimney because of convection.

10

See for yourself!

1 Make yourself a convection detector! Start by drawing a coiled snake on a sheet of stiff paper or thin cardboard.

2 Color your snake, and use a pair of scissors to cut it out carefully along the curved lines.

3 Tie a piece of thread through a small hole in the snake's head, and dangle it over a radiator.

Fine string or thread

4 The warm air rising pushes on the underside of the coils and makes the snake spin. The warmer the air, the faster the snake will spin.

Rising warm air

WOW!

Roman radiators

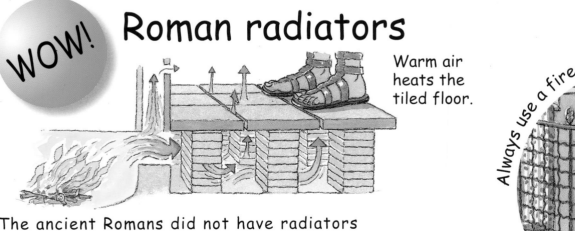

Warm air heats the tiled floor.

The ancient Romans did not have radiators **on** their walls. Their radiators **were** the walls (and the floors). A big furnace heated the air, and the hot air then traveled through channels under the floor and behind the walls.

Always use a fire screen in front of the fireplace.

What does polishing do?

What do aliens use to polish floors?

Science friction!

You can see your reflection in the surface of a polished, wood table because it is smooth and shiny. Rough, unpolished wood looks dull, and when you touch it, you can feel tiny bits of wood sticking out and catching your skin. If you push two smooth surfaces over each other, they slide easily. But it is difficult to slide two rough surfaces against each other because they grip onto each other. This resistance to sliding is caused by a force called *friction*. Polishing a table not only cleans the surface, but it also stops friction, protecting the surface from objects.

Smoothing surfaces

Rubbing wood with sandpaper gets rid of any rough bits and makes the surface smoother.

Rough   Smoother

Polish

Wax polish fills tiny holes in a surface, making it level. It also helps form a protective coating.

Rough surfaces catch on each other. There is friction.

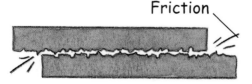

Friction

Smooth surfaces do not catch on each other. There is no friction.

See for yourself!

**1** Find a big, wood toy brick. Tape a piece of smooth tinfoil on the top and a piece of rough sandpaper on the bottom.

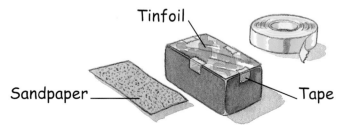

Tinfoil

Sandpaper

Tape

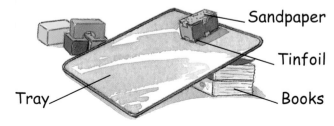**2** Prop up a tray or cookie sheet to create a gentle slope. Put the brick at the top of the slope, with its shiny surface down.

Sandpaper

Tinfoil

Tray

Books

3 Does the brick slide down, or does friction stop it? If the brick does not move, gradually make the slope steeper until it starts to slide. How steep is the slope?

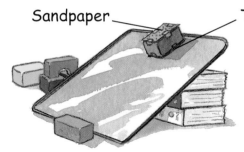

Sandpaper

Tinfoil

Add more books to make the slope steeper.

4 Do the same with the rough surface of the brick face down. You will have to make the slope much steeper before the brick will slide. The sandpaper causes more friction.

Tinfoil

Sandpaper

WOW!

Speedy skis!

Although most of us would find ice and snow very slippery already, racing skiers put wax on the bottom of their skis so that they can go even faster.

Don't put rugs on a polished floor!

13

Who's in the family portrait?

Ever looked at a family portrait and noticed that you look like your relatives? This is because we are all made of *cells*. Inside cells are thousands of *genes*, chemical instructions that tell cells how to grow. Half a baby's genes come from its father and half from its mother, who in turn got their genes from their parents. Genes affect what we look like and how our bodies develop. We all have a different mixture of genes (except for *identical twins*), so we all look different.

> Why does Marie look like her sister?

> Because they have the same jeans!

Eye colors

Some genes have a stronger effect than other genes. For example, if you have a gene for brown eyes, you will have brown eyes, even if you have a gene for blue eyes as well.

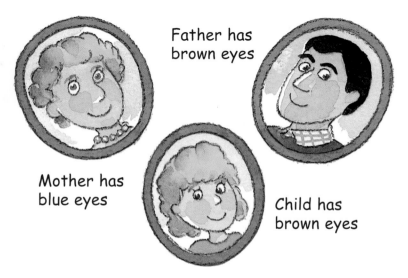

Mother has blue eyes

Father has brown eyes

Child has brown eyes

Grandmother has blue eyes

Your parents might have brown eyes but, if they both have a blue-eyed parent, you may have blue eyes.

See for yourself!

1 Think about yourself. What things do you do well? Is there anyone in your family who is good at the same things? It could be a brother, sister, or parent, or it might be an uncle, aunt, or grandparent.

2 Look at yourself in the mirror or in a photo. What does your face look like? Look at old family photos. See if you have the same eyes or nose as one of your relatives.

Some of your genes will be the same as the person you look like.

3 Do you have any identical twins in your family or in your school? Why do you think they are identical?

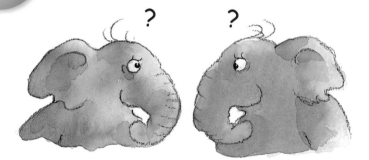

Cool cats!

Siamese cats

WOW!

In some animals, including Siamese cats and Himalayan rabbits, the genes that make the fur grow dark only work in the cooler parts of their bodies. The tips of their noses, tails, paws, and ears are dark, and the rest of their fur is pale.

Himalayan rabbit

Make the most of your genes—practice!

What is a photo?

When you take a photo, the *lens* at the front of the camera allows light to fall on a film inside the camera. The film you use to take a photo is coated with chemicals that change when light shines on them. They are affected by the energy in light and go darker, making a *negative* picture. The film then has to be "developed." This means it is treated with other chemicals, so you can see the picture.

What do mice say when you take their photo?

Cheese!

Developing a photo

When the film is finished, the roll is taken out of the camera. All of the developing and printing has to be done in the dark. The film is developed into a negative.

To print the photo, light is shone through the negative onto a sheet of photographic paper, which has been treated with chemicals.

The film is taken out of the camera and developed into a strip of negatives.

Negative

In the negative, light and dark are the wrong way around.

Developing bath

Now, the print is positive, with light and dark in the right places.

Printed photo

16

See for yourself! ✋

1 To see how a picture is projected onto the film, you can make a pinhole camera from a shoebox. Get an adult to cut a big window in one end.

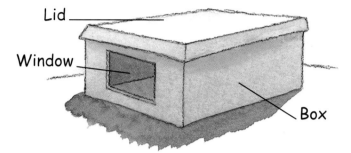

Lid

Window

Box

2 Tape wax paper over the window. This makes a screen where the film would be in a real camera.

Wax paper

Tape

3 Ask an adult to make a small hole in the middle of the other end with a thin skewer. This is where the camera lens would be.

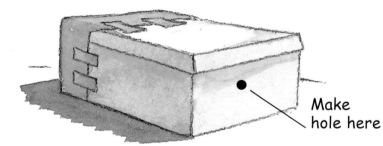

Make hole here

4 Point the "camera" at a bright lamp in a dark room. When you get it in the right position, you can see the shape of the light on the paper screen.

Image

Seeing through you!

WOW!

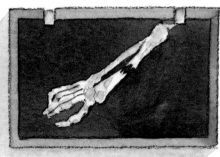

X rays do not go through the bone.

X-ray machines give off rays that can go through soft materials, such as skin, but not hard materials, such as bone. This means that in an X-ray photo, broken bones show up clearly.

Keep unused film away from the light.

What is newspaper made of?

All paper, whether it is fine tissue paper, cardboard, or newspaper, is a web of tough plant *fibers* made into a flat sheet. The fibers can be chopped up and used to make paper, but, first, any unwanted parts of the plant have to be broken down by chemicals and washed away. Newspapers are printed on paper made of *wood pulp* from fast-growing trees, such as pine.

What's black and white and red all over?

A newspaper!

How paper is made

Paper can be made by hand, but most of it is made in a factory called a paper mill. Paper mills can also *recycle* old newspapers and other paper.

Pine trees

Pulp

Wood chips

Wood chips are ground up by machines and mixed with water to make a soft mixture called pulp.

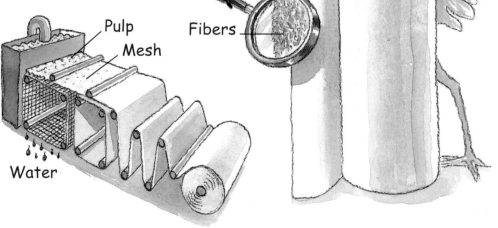

Pulp

Mesh

Water

Fibers

The pulp is poured onto a mesh frame, which allows the water to drain away.

It is pressed and dried to make long rolls of paper—you can see the fibers in any piece of paper.

18

See for yourself!

1 Tear three sheets of scrap paper into very small pieces. Add a cup of water, and soak them for about two hours.

Water

2 Cut out a piece of stiff mesh or embroidery canvas, and attach it to a small frame, using tape or thumbtacks.

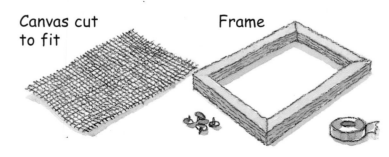

Canvas cut to fit

Frame

3 Mash the torn paper into pulp using a fork or an egg beater. Or ask an adult to liquidize it in a blender. The pulp should look like thick soup. Spread it evenly over the mesh.

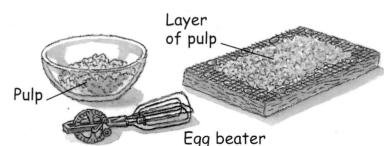

Layer of pulp

Pulp

Egg beater

4 Take the mesh off the frame and place it, pulp side down, on a dry dishcloth. Press down to squeeze out most of the water. Leave it to dry in a warm place, then peel the paper off the mesh.

A rolling pin helps to squeeze out water.

Wasp news!

WOW!

Animals were making paper long before humans were able to. Some wasps chew wood into a pulp, then use it to build their nests. It is surprisingly strong and weatherproof. Inside are papery cells, like a honeycomb, where wasp larvae live.

Keep waste paper for recycling.

How do things get dusty?

Have you ever wondered how dust gets everywhere? Your feet may track mud into the house and make floors dirty, but other surfaces get dusty, too. A lot of dust blows in from the air outside, especially in windy weather. If you live in a town or city, the air is full of *particles* from cars, chimneys, and road surfaces. In other places, the air contains sand from deserts, salt from the sea, soil from farms and gardens, and even chemicals from factories. All of these things help make dust.

Why did the cleaner stop cleaning?

Because grime didn't pay!

Homemade dust

Not all dust comes from outside. You make some of it yourself.

Dust

Animals make dust too— they shed little bits of fur and feathers as well as skin.

Run your finger along a high shelf or cabinet. The dust you pick up with your finger is skin you made weeks ago.

Skin

As new skin grows on your body, little flakes of old skin wear away and fall off.

See for yourself!

1 Find a place with a clear beam of light, either from a sunny window or a lamp.

Beam of light

2 Take off one of your socks, and shake it across the beam. You will see tiny specks of skin dancing in the light. They are being pushed around by invisible movements of the air.

Specks of skin

3 Large particles of dust are pulled down to the ground by *gravity*, but the air pushes a lot of fine dust sideways and even up onto other surfaces.

Cotton swab

Use damp cotton swabs to test surfaces, like walls and mirrors, for dust.

Long-distance dust!

When a volcano erupts, it may throw dust high into the air. This can travel for miles in the atmosphere before coming down in a faraway place. The dust may even block out so much sunlight that the weather can change, making temperatures cooler.

WOW!

Don't breathe in too much dust—it can make you sneeze!

How does the light switch on?

Electricity is a useful kind of energy that can be made in one place and used somewhere else. It flows as an *electric current* from one place to the other along a metal wire. Metal is a *conductor* because it lets electricity pass through it. Millions of electrons stream into the wire at one end and out at the other. On its way, the current can make a bulb light up.

What stays inside when you put it out?

The light!

Lighting up

When electricity can flow all the way around a wire, we say there is a complete *circuit*.

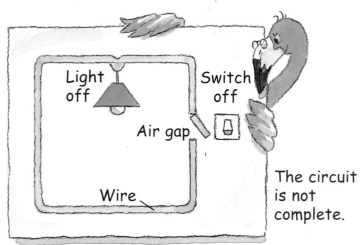

Light off
Switch off
Air gap
Wire
The circuit is not complete.

If the light switch is off, there is a gap in the wire, which the electrons cannot jump across. Unlike metal, air is not a conductor.

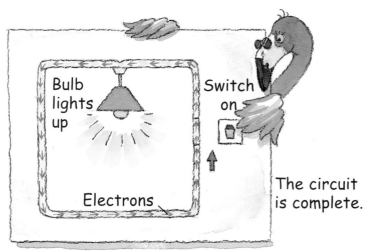

Bulb lights up
Switch on
Electrons
The circuit is complete.

When the light switch is on, the gap in the wire is closed. The circuit is complete, and the light comes on.

See for yourself!

1 To see how a switch works, tape a piece of fuse wire to the negative end of a AA battery (the one without the knob). Make sure metal is touching metal.

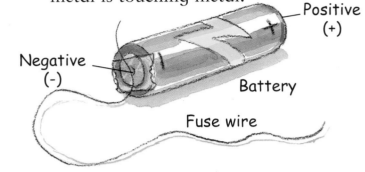

Positive (+)

Negative (-)

Battery

Fuse wire

2 Now wrap the other end of the wire around the base of a flashlight bulb. The bulb will not come on yet because the circuit is not complete.

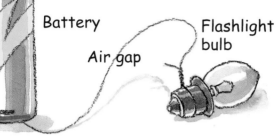

Battery

Air gap

Flashlight bulb

3 Complete the circuit by touching the positive end of the battery with the bottom of the bulb. The light comes on.

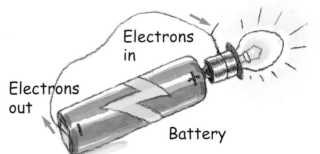

Electrons in

Electrons out

Battery

The electrons flow out of the bottom, through the wire, and in at the top.

4 You can try lighting up a dollhouse. You can buy bulb holders, wire, and switches from toy stores.

NEVER touch a fuse box!

Dim the lights!

WOW!

Dimmer switches can reduce the light without switching it off completely. They make it more difficult for the electrons to get through the circuit.

How can plants grow indoors?

Plants that are grown indoors must be given everything they would have outdoors. They need light to give them energy to grow, the right kind of soil, the right amount of water, and warmth. Some plants like to be in the sunshine all day, others like to be in a shady spot. Sun-loving plants are harder to grow in the house. In their natural habitat, many plants that do well indoors would grow under trees and in other shady places.

Why can't you trust trees?

Because they can be a bit shady!

Happy houseplants

Room lighting is not as bright as sunlight, but ivy, ferns, and green, leafy aspidistras can grow well in dim artifical light.

Aspidistra

Fern

Ivy

Geranium

Cactus

Other plants won't flower if they don't have enough sunlight.

Air plant

Air plants do not need soil. They grow on tree bark and are kept moist by spraying.

See for yourself!

1 Try growing your own plants. Find a nice bushy geranium plant or a carnation with plenty of side shoots.

Geranium   Carnation

2 Take "cuttings" by breaking off some of the small shoots that do not have flowers. Gently pull off the lower leaves, so you have at least 2 inches (5cm) of bare stem.

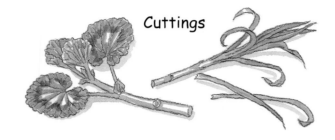

Cuttings

3 Place the bare stems into a pot of damp soil, and put them on a sunny windowsill. Keep the cuttings damp and warm until some of them produce roots and start to grow.

4 Move the cuttings into separate pots. Return one to the sunny windowsill and put another in a dark corner. Compare how they grow.

Which plant do you think grew on the windowsill?

Fungus farms

WOW!

Only green plants need light to grow. Mushrooms are fungi, not green plants. They are "farmed" in the dark, because they get their energy from the rotting compost in which they are grown.

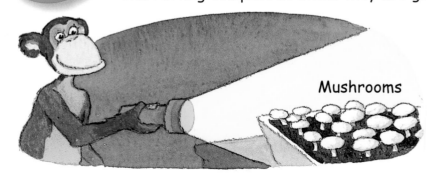

Mushrooms

Remember to take care of your plants.

How can I speak on the phone?

When you talk to a friend face-to-face, *sound energy* comes from your mouth and travels straight through the air to your friend's ear. If you and your friend are farther apart, the energy cannot travel far enough through the air, so you use a telephone instead. This changes the *vibrations* from your voice into *electrical signals*, which can travel long distances. Cellular and cordless phones turn sound vibrations into other forms of energy.

How do elephants speak to each other?

By 'elephone!

From sound to signal

The telephone mouthpiece converts the sounds you make into electric currents.

The vibrations cause changes in a tiny electric current leaving your phone.

Your friend's telephone earpiece is like a little loudspeaker. It converts the electrical signals back into sound.

Disk vibrates to give sound.

Mouthpiece

Wire

Earpiece

Vibrating air makes the mouthpiece vibrate.

These are the electrical signals that flow down the telephone line to your friend's phone.

26

See for yourself! ✋

1 To make a model telephone, ask an adult to make a small hole in the bottom of two plastic cups or yogurt containers.

Cups

2 Thread both cups onto a long piece of string. Tie a knot at both ends of the string.

String

Knot

Knot

3 Stand far apart so that the string is tight. Put your phone to your ear and get your friend to speak loudly into theirs. Can you feel the vibrations?

4 Now you speak. Can you feel the vibrations from your voice going into the phone? If the string is too loose, the vibrations cannot travel along it.

You must keep the string tight.

WOW! Laser lines

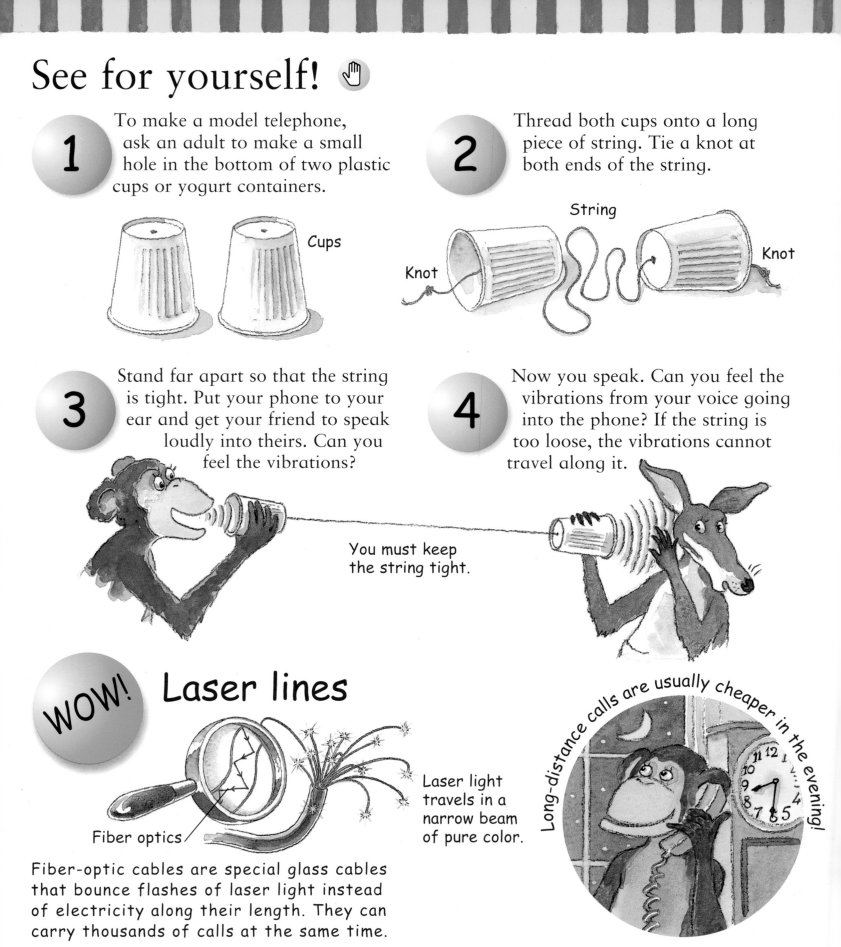

Fiber optics

Laser light travels in a narrow beam of pure color.

Fiber-optic cables are special glass cables that bounce flashes of laser light instead of electricity along their length. They can carry thousands of calls at the same time.

Long-distance calls are usually cheaper in the evening!

27

How do speakers work?

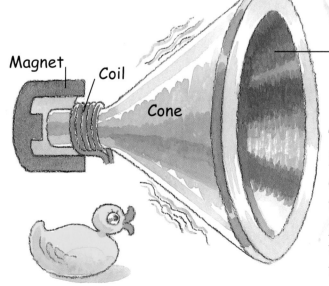

Why is a radio never complete?

Because it is wireless!

Radios, CD players, televisions, telephones—anything that runs on electricity and lets you hear music and voices will have a speaker. Some speakers are big, some are tiny, but they all turn electrical signals into sound. Vibrations in the speaker move the air, which in turn makes your *eardrum*, and then the inside of your ear, vibrate. Your ear sends a message to your brain, which unscrambles the sound.

Sound waves

Most speakers contain a coil of metal wire, a magnet, and a cone-shaped piece of paper or plastic.

Magnet

Coil

Cone

Vibrations

To make a sound, little pulses of electricity are sent to the coil. The pulses work with the magnet to make the coil vibrate.

These vibrations move from the coil to the cone and through the air around it. They travel through the air as *sound waves*.

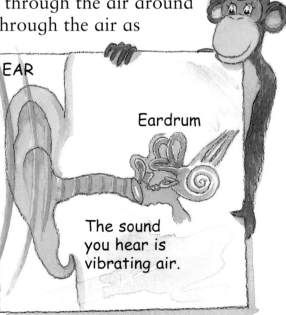

EAR

Eardrum

The sound you hear is vibrating air.

See for yourself!

1 See how sound makes your eardrum vibrate. You will need a wide, strong cardboard tube with two open ends, a balloon, some plastic wrap, some rubber bands, a sequin, and some glue.

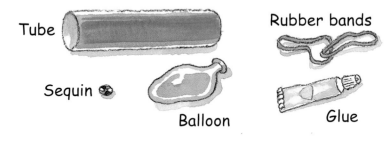

Tube

Sequin

Balloon

Rubber bands

Glue

2 Completely cover one end of the tube with a piece of balloon or plastic wrap. Stretch it tightly and attach it firmly with rubber bands or tape. Glue the sequin just off center.

Sequin stuck on

Balloon stretched tight

3 Hold the tube so that the sequin just catches a beam of light from a desk lamp and reflects onto a wall. Then toot down the tube and watch the reflection vibrate.

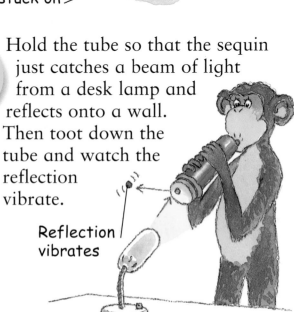

Reflection vibrates

Woofers and tweeters

WOW!

Tweeter

Woofer

Stereo speakers have big "woofers" for lower sounds and small "tweeters" for higher sounds. Tweeters can vibrate faster than woofers.

Be careful—loud sounds can damage your ears!

Living Room quiz

1 What do you get if you mix red and green light?
a) Blue
b) Yellow
c) Black

2 What happens when you sit down on a foam cushion?
a) It is compressed
b) It feels hard
c) It floats up

3 What happens to the hot air just above the radiator?
a) It sinks
b) It rises
c) It turns to steam

4 Why do skiers put wax on the bottom of their skis?
a) To go faster
b) To stop quickly
c) To keep their feet warm

5 What does the telephone turn sound into?
a) Convection currents
b) Morse code
c) Electric currents

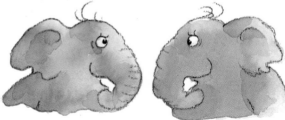

6 What changes the film inside a camera?
a) Light
b) Dark
c) Sound

7 What are newspapers made from?
a) Coal
b) Wood pulp
c) Wool

8 What do you call a metal that carries an electric current?
a) An electron
b) A conductor
c) A circuit

9 What plants like to be in the shade?
a) Ferns
b) Cacti
c) Geraniums

10 Where would you find a "woofer"?
a) In a telephone
b) In a sofa
c) In a stereo

30

Answers on page 32

Glossary

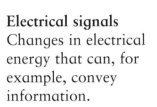

Cells
The tiny living units that make up our bodies.

Circuit
The path taken by an electric current through a conductor.

Conduction
The movement of energy (heat or electricity) through a material that does not move itself.

Conductor
A material that allows heat or electricity to pass through it.

Convection
The movement of heat through a liquid or gas, carried by currents of heated particles.

Eardrum
The thin partition between the outer ear and the middle ear that vibrates when sound waves hit it.

Elastic
Able to stretch and then return to the original shape and size.

Electric current
The flow of electrical energy through a conductor.

Electrical signals
Changes in electrical energy that can, for example, convey information.

Electrons
Tiny particles that carry electrical energy.

Energy
The ability to do work or make something happen.

Fibers
Thin, threadlike structures in plants that help support them and hold them upright.

Force
A push or pull that changes something's movement or shape.

Friction
The force that tries to stop two surfaces from sliding over each other.

Genes
Chemical instructions, passed on from parents to their children, which control what a person is like.

Gravity
The pull from the earth that makes things fall down.

Heat energy
Energy that moves between two things if one is hotter than the other.

Identical twins
Twins who have exactly the same genes, who are the same sex, and who look alike.

Lens
A piece of transparent material with curved surfaces that can bend the path of light passing through it.

Negative
A picture, usually on transparent plastic, on which the areas that should be dark are light, and those that should be light are dark.

Particles
Very tiny parts or small pieces of something.

Phosphor
A substance that gives out light when hit again and again by energy from electrons.

Radiation
Rays of energy, such as heat or light, given off from a source and traveling through air or space.

Recycle
To collect and process materials that have been used before, so that they can be used again.

Sound energy
Energy carried by sound waves.

Sound waves
Disturbances moving through the air that make the eardrum vibrate, producing the sensation of hearing.

Tuned
A receiver is tuned when it produces the best possible response to a signal coming in.

Vibrations
Back-and-forth movements around a middle position.

Wood pulp
Wood that has been broken down into a pulp.

Index

Answers to the Living Room quiz on page 30
1 b **2** a **3** b **4** a **5** c **6** a **7** b **8** b **9** a **10** c